# Great Masters:
# Stravinsky—His Life and Music
## Robert Greenberg, Ph.D.

**PUBLISHED BY:**

**THE TEACHING COMPANY**
4840 Westfields Boulevard, Suite 500
Chantilly, Virginia 20151-2299
1-800-TEACH-12
Fax—703-378-3819
www.teach12.com

Copyright © The Teaching Company, 2000

Printed in the United States of America

This book is in copyright. All rights reserved.

Without limiting the rights under copyright reserved above,
no part of this publication may be reproduced, stored in
or introduced into a retrieval system, or transmitted,
in any form, or by any means
(electronic, mechanical, photocopying, recording, or otherwise),
without the prior written permission of
The Teaching Company.

# Robert Greenberg, Ph.D.

Chairman, Department of Music History and Literature
San Francisco Conservatory of Music

Robert Greenberg has composed over forty works for a wide variety of instrumental and vocal ensembles. Recent performances of Greenberg's work have taken place in New York, San Francisco, Los Angeles, Chicago, England, Ireland, Italy, Greece, and The Netherlands, where his *Child's Play* for string quartet was performed at the Concertgebouw of Amsterdam in 1993.

Professor Greenberg holds degrees from Princeton University and the University of California at Berkeley, where he received a Ph.D. in music composition in 1984. His principal teachers were Edward Cone, Claudio Spies, Andrew Imbrie, and Olly Wilson.

Professor Greenberg's awards include three Nicola De Lorenzo prizes in composition, three Meet the Composer grants, and commissions from the Koussevitzky Foundation of the Library of Congress, the Alexander String Quartet, XTET, the San Francisco Contemporary Music Players, and the Dancer's Stage Ballet Company.

He is currently on the faculty of the San Francisco Conservatory of Music, where he is Chair of the Department of Music History and Literature and Director of Curriculum of the Adult Extension Division.

Professor Greenberg is creator, host, and lecturer for the San Francisco Symphony's Discovery Series. The Discovery Series is a special subscription series in which participants attend four 3-hour lectures over the course of the concert season on topics that are geared to the repertoire under performance.

Professor Greenberg has taught and lectured extensively across North American and Europe, speaking to such corporations and musical institutions as Arthur Andersen and Andersen Consulting, Diamond Technologies, Canadian Pacific, Strategos Institute, Lincoln Center, the Van Cliburn Foundation, the University of California/Haas School of Business Executive Seminar, the Commonwealth Club of San Francisco, and others. His work as a teacher and lecturer has been profiled in the *Wall Street Journal*, *Inc.* magazine, the *San Francisco Chronicle*, and the *Times of London*. He is an artistic codirector and board member of

COMPOSER, INC. His music is published by Fallen Leaf Press and CPP/Belwin and is recorded on the Innova Label.

# Table of Contents
# Great Masters:
# Stravinsky—His Life and Music

**Professor Biography** ..................................................................... i
**Course Scope** .............................................................................. 1
**Lecture One**         Introduction and There's No Place
                        Like Home ......................................................... 5
**Lecture Two**         From Student to Professional ........................... 10
**Lecture Three**       *The Rite of Spring* ............................................. 15
**Lecture Four**        The War Years (WWI) ..................................... 19
**Lecture Five**        Neoclassicism .................................................. 23
**Lecture Six**         Maturity ........................................................... 27
**Lecture Seven**       A Citizen of the World ..................................... 31
**Lecture Eight**       The New Stravinsky ......................................... 36
**Vocal Texts** ............................................................................... 41
**Timeline** .................................................................................... 44
**Glossary** .................................................................................... 46
**Biographical Notes** ................................................................... 48
**Bibliography** ............................................................................. 50

# Great Masters:
# Stravinsky—His Life and Music

**Scope:**

Igor Stravinsky composed what is arguably one of the two most important pieces of 20th-century music: *The Rite of Spring*. (The other work is Arnold Schoenberg's *Pierrot Lunaire*.) Both works helped to revolutionize the musical language of the 20th century and offered models to countless other composers for their own creative work. Stravinsky's creative life, however, cannot be defined by *The Rite of Spring* alone. He was, in many ways, unique in the diversity and originality of his stylistic development. If we want to understand Stravinsky's musical development, we must appreciate the crucial and substantial influence exerted by his childhood in St. Petersburg (Petrograd/Leningrad). In this city at the turn of the 20th century, the young and impressionable Stravinsky was exposed to an amazing, kaleidoscopic interweaving of Western and Eastern European cultures. Diversity, synthesis, and reconciliation are the keys to Stravinsky's musical personality. Stravinsky was privileged to receive the benefits of an upper-middle-class Russian upbringing. His was a musical family. His father, Fyodor, was a professional opera singer, considered one of the great bass-baritones of his day. By his late teens, Stravinsky's interest in music had developed into an ambition to become a composer, despite the fact that he had not, to that point of his life, demonstrated any exceptional musical talent. Certainly, his potential was not recognized by the eminent Russian composer Nicolai Rimsky-Korsakov, when Stravinsky approached him for lessons in 1902. Rimsky-Korsakov's opinion changed dramatically, however, when he heard Stravinsky's Piano Sonata in F Sharp Minor of 1904. The work gained Stravinsky a powerful ally and influential teacher in that great Russian master. Between 1904 and 1909, Stravinsky developed his compositional technique and style, absorbing a diversity of musical influences, including the music of the Russian nationalists and the contemporary French composer Claude Debussy. During this period, Stravinsky married his cousin Katya, who would prove an invaluable support to her husband during these musically formative and professionally difficult years. In 1909, Stravinsky's life took a hugely significant turn when he met the brilliant impresario Serge Diaghilev, who was about to launch his new ballet company, the *Ballets Russes* (Russian Ballet). By this time, Stravinsky had established himself as a composer of talent. Diaghilev commissioned him to arrange some piano pieces by Chopin for orchestra. For the second season of the *Ballets Russes*, Diaghilev commissioned Stravinsky to write the score for a new ballet based on a Russian folktale, *The Firebird*. This work, which melds traditional Russian nationalist elements with Stravinsky's own innovations, was a triumph.

Although Stravinsky's audiences enjoyed his highly successful music for *The Firebird* and his next ballet, *Petrushka*, they could not have anticipated what would come next. Stravinsky's music for *The Rite of Spring*, again composed for the *Ballets Russes*, was like nothing he or any other composer had written before it. To convey the sense of the ballet's primitive, earthy, and sexual theme, Stravinsky had to forge a new musical language. The resultant ballet score caused one of the most celebrated scandals in music history. At *The Rite*'s Paris premiere on May 29, 1913, the audience broke into a riot. This music still sounds "modern" almost a century after its first performance.

Although Stravinsky never composed another work like *The Rite of Spring*, the compositional techniques he used in it would remain central to his music for the rest of his long life. World War I forced economies of means on Stravinsky, with the result that the works he composed from 1914 to 1918 were, on the whole, constructed on a much smaller scale than the ballets *Firebird*, *Petrushka*, and *The Rite of Spring*. They also employed a less brutal, less dissonant musical language than *The Rite*. Among the compositions of these years were *Renard* (*The Fox*) for four voices and small orchestra (1916), *Ragtime for Eleven Instruments* (1918), and the great masterpiece of the period, *Les Noces* (*The Wedding*), finished in 1923.

During these years, Stravinsky and his wife, Katya, were living in Switzerland. After 1914, he would not return to Russia for another forty-eight years. World War I left Stravinsky depressed and virtually destitute. Because of the Russian Revolution and the contemporary copyright law situation, he received nothing for performances of *The Firebird*, his most popular work written to that time. As a result, he began a lifelong habit of re-orchestrating his most popular works to ensure his maintenance of copyright ownership.

One of the cultural legacies of the period immediately following World War I was a nostalgic hearkening back to seemingly more humane times. With his usual commercial acumen, Diaghilev took advantage of this nostalgia to propose a ballet to Stravinsky that would be based on the music of the 18th-century composer Pergolesi. Entitled *Pulcinella*, this work became Stravinsky's door to the musical past. He created a score that was not merely Pergolesi re-arranged and re-orchestrated but a brilliant synthesis of Pergolesi's melodies and his own unique brand of harmonic, rhythmic, and orchestral expression.

By the mid-1920s, Stravinsky was composing music that was governed by purely formal considerations, in his words, without "literary" or "picturesque" associations, and music almost devoid of expressive nuance. According to Stravinsky himself, the essential compositional process in these works was counterpoint. This new style is exemplified by the Octet for Winds of 1923 and the Piano Sonata of 1925, the year in which he made a highly successful tour of several U.S. cities, conducting his own works.

Through the end of the 1920s, Stravinsky continued to produce music that filtered its modernisms through the lens of the musical past, such as the ballet *Apollo Musagète* of 1928 and *The Symphony of Psalms* of 1930. Commissioned by the Boston Symphony Orchestra, *The Symphony of Psalms* is a deeply religious work, of the sort that Stravinsky had never written before. Among the events that may have led to Stravinsky's newly expressed spirituality was the death of his friend, champion, and sparring partner, Diaghilev, in Venice in 1928. Musically, even by Stravinsky's standards, *The Symphony of Psalms* uses an extreme economy of means.

The works of the 1930s continued to exhibit the same sort of neoclassical, or neotonal, style as the earlier Piano Sonata and *The Symphony of Psalms*. These works included the Concerto in D for Violin and the *Dumbarton Oaks* Concerto, among others. The latter work was commissioned in 1937 by Mr. and Mrs. Robert Woods Bliss of Washington, D.C., where it was premiered the following year.

The years 1938 to 1939 were memorable ones for Stravinsky, for both happy and tragic reasons. They began with another commission from Mr. and Mrs. Robert Woods Bliss. (The work would eventually become the *Symphony in C*.) Stravinsky was also invited to deliver lectures for the Harvard Norton lecture series. In the meantime, however, his music was being attacked as "degenerate art" by the Nazis in Germany, and he suffered the multiple tragedy of the deaths of his daughter, Lyudmilla, his wife, Katya, and his mother.

When World War II broke out in September 1939, Stravinsky and his girlfriend and soon-to-be second wife, Vera Sudeykin, arrived in the United

States, there to honor his commitment to Harvard University. In March 1940, Igor and Vera were married. Because the war in Europe made return to Paris impossible, they settled in Los Angeles, where Stravinsky immediately became one of the city's most sought-after celebrities. His first major work composed in the United States was his "War Symphony," the *Symphony in Three Movements*.

The *Symphony in Three Movements* was completed in 1945, the year that the Stravinskys became American citizens. Among other works Stravinsky wrote between 1945 and 1953 was the *Ebony* Concerto, written for Woody Herman's band. This work "objectifies" elements of jazz in the way that *Ragtime for Eleven Wind Instruments* had twenty years before.

These years were perhaps the best of Stravinsky's life: he was happy and flourishing in both his private and his professional lives; financial hardship was a thing of the past. In 1948, Stravinsky befriended Robert Craft, a young conductor with a fanatical admiration for the older composer. Theirs became a highly unusual relationship, in which Craft wrote diaries of his life as Stravinsky's aide and friend. Craft introduced Stravinsky to the twelve-tone music of Schoenberg, Berg, and Webern. In his seventies, Stravinsky was inspired to begin a new musical journey that would transform his musical language more radically than ever before.

Stravinsky had no difficulty absorbing Schoenberg's highly intellectualized and formulaic serial music. Stravinsky's ballet music *Agon*, composed between 1953 and 1957, exemplifies his new style with its mixture of neotonal and serial elements.

After the Stravinskys and Robert Craft returned from their landmark visit to Russia in 1962, Stravinsky's output began to slow down. The bulk of his compositions from 1957 to 1966 were liturgical, including the *Requiem Canticles*, his last major work and the most accessible of his late works.

By the late 1960s, Stravinsky was enjoying a level of celebrity and wealth rarely accorded a composer in his lifetime. In 1967, he made his last public appearance. Two years later, for medical reasons, he moved to New York City, where he died on April 6, 1971. He was buried on the island of San Michele in Venice, his favorite city, near the grave of Serge Diaghilev. Vera was buried beside him twelve years later.

# Lecture One
# Introduction and There's No Place Like Home

**Scope:** Igor Stravinsky's extraordinary musical originality and stylistic diversity was a direct outgrowth of his intense and profoundly rich childhood. Stravinsky was born into an upper-middle-class Russian family in 1882. His father, Fyodor, was one of the great Russian operatic bass-baritones of his time. The St. Petersburg in which Igor grew up was an amazing mix of Western and Eastern Europe—not so much a "clash" of unlike parts as a single, faceted whole. This confrontation of East and West is a key to understanding Stravinsky's musical development. For the most part, Stravinsky's parents did little to encourage his musical ambitions. In 1899, Fyodor Stravinsky slipped and fell during an opera performance. Subsequently, he developed a fatal cancer. Stravinsky was accepted into law school despite a mediocre academic record. He also continued his music lessons. Although the great Russian composer Nicolai Rimsky-Korsakov delivered a discouraging assessment of his compositions, Stravinsky remained undeterred in his ambition to become a composer. In 1902, Fyodor Stravinsky died and Igor's adulthood began.

## Outline

**I.** We begin by comparing music by Mozart and Tchaikovsky with music by Stravinsky.

   **A.** Do we have a problem recognizing that the following three excerpts were written by the same person—someone living in the late 18th century? **Musical examples:** Mozart's Symphony No. 9 in C Major, K. 73 (1769), Movement 4; Mozart's Symphony No. 29 in A Major (1774), K. 201, Movement 4; Mozart's Symphony No. 41 in C Major, K. 551 (1788), Movement 4.

   **B.** Do we have a problem recognizing the following three excerpts as written by the same person—someone living in the late 19th century? **Musical examples:** Tchaikovsky's Symphony No. 2 in C Minor, Op. 17 (1872), Movement 4; Tchaikovsky's Symphony No. 4 in F Minor, Op. 36 (1877), Movement 4; Tchaikovsky's Symphony No. 6 in B Minor, Op. 74 (1893), Movement 3.

C. The following five excerpts from music by the 20th-century composer Stravinsky, on the other hand, reveal a kaleidoscopic variety of musical styles and expression. **Musical examples:** *Firebird* (1910), "Khorovode Dance No. 1"; *The Rite of Spring* (1912), "Dance of the Earth"; *Pulcinella* (1920), Overture; *Ebony* Concerto (1945), Movement 3; *Abraham and Isaac* (1963).

II. Stravinsky began his compositional life as a 19th-century musical nationalist.
   A. He was a student of the great Russian composer Nicolai Rimsky-Korsakov.
   B. He became the *enfant terrible* of modern music before World War I.
   C. After the war, he turned to the musical styles of seemingly simpler, more "humane" times.
   D. From the 1920s to the 1940s, he wrote music in such popular idioms as ragtime, tango, and big-band jazz.
   E. During the 1950s and 1960s, he underwent another compositional transformation and began composing in an ultra-modern style—a style created and popularized by composers one-third his age.
   F. Was Stravinsky simply a musical opportunist or a chameleon without a genuine musical personality of his own? Or was he a supreme original, whose essential compositional tools remained more or less the same during his long career, despite the changing "style" of his music?

III. Stravinsky's extraordinary musical originality radiates outward from his childhood.
   A. Stravinsky was born on June 17, 1882, in Oranienbaum, now known as Lomonosov, on the Gulf of Finland, about thirty-five miles west of St. Petersburg.
   B. His parents came from minor nobility whose family fortunes had declined.
   C. Stravinsky's father, Fyodor, was one of the great Russian bass-baritones of his time.

1. Fyodor's career coincided with the golden age of Russian opera.
2. His portrayal of Varlaam contributed to the huge success of the 1896 revival of Mussorgsky's *Boris Godunov*. **Musical example:** Modest Mussorgsky, *Boris Godunov* (1874), Varlaam's Song.
3. In 1876, Fyodor became a member of the Imperial Theater in St. Petersburg, where he remained until his retirement in 1902.

**D.** The St. Petersburg in which Stravinsky grew up was a unique melange of East and West.
1. The city was an amazing mix of Western and Eastern Europe, of rich and poor, of city people and country peasantry.
2. It was also the dirtiest, most diseased, and most overcrowded capital city in Europe.
3. The exotic confrontation of East and West is a key to understanding Stravinsky's musical development.
4. The cultural mayhem of St. Petersburg was not so much a "clash" of unlike parts as it was a single, faceted whole that was greater than its parts.
5. An adult observing St. Petersburg for the first time at the turn of the 20th century would be aware of the confrontation of unlike parts; a child growing up in such an environment, however, would see it as being part of a greater whole, interconnected, related, and interdependent.

**E.** Stravinsky hated school, made few friends, and was a poor student.
1. Fyodor Stravinsky spent tremendous sums of money on tutors to prepare his son for his university entrance exams.
2. Although Stravinsky's parents were not enthusiastic about their son's interest in music, Stravinsky began studying piano at the age of nine or ten.
3. At this time, he began to attend operas, mostly by Russian composers but also by Mozart, Wagner, Meyerbeer, Verdi, Rossini, Bizet (*Carmen*), and Gounod (*Faust*).
4. He would also have heard concerts of orchestral and chamber music dominated by the Russian repertoire.

5. By the age of seventeen, Stravinsky had a spotty musical education at best. He was a competent pianist and good sight-reader, but his aspirations, in the eyes of his father, clearly outstripped his abilities.

IV. Two events occurred in 1899 that would shape Stravinsky's future,

   A. In 1899, Stravinsky, having decided to become a composer, wanted theory and composition lessons.
      1. Stravinsky's parents "compromised" by finding him a "real" piano teacher, Leokadiya Alexandrovna Kashperova.
      2. Leokadiya was a former student of the great Anton Rubinstein.
      3. Stravinsky resigned himself to a strict regimen of technical piano exercises.
   B. During the spring of 1899, Fyodor Stravinsky fell during a performance.
      1. He began to suffer intense back pain that would soon reveal itself to be cancer.
      2. From 1899 to 1902, Fyodor's illness dominated his family's life.
      3. Igor was unwilling to push a musical agenda that went against his sick father's wishes.

V. In 1901, Stravinsky was accepted into the University of St. Petersburg as a law student, but he continued his music lessons.

   A. He began music theory with St. Petersburg Conservatory graduates, former students of Rimsky-Korsakov.
   B. Among Stravinsky's classmates was Vladimir (Volodya) Rimsky-Korsakov, a competent violinist and violist and the youngest son of the composer.
      1. Volodya urged Stravinsky to show his compositions to his father.
      2. Rimsky-Korsakov advised Stravinsky to continue his studies in harmony and counterpoint under systematic supervision.
      3. He stated that he would be willing to take Stravinsky "in hand" when he had "acquired the necessary foundation."
      4. Stravinsky was not deterred.

5. He rapidly made friends with the rest of the Rimsky-Korsakov clan, who soon constituted almost a second family for him.

VI. In November 1902, four months after Igor's meeting with Rimsky-Korsakov, Fyodor Stravinsky died.
   A. His father's death removed the main obstacle to Stravinsky's ambition to become a composer.
   B. Thus, in November 1920, at the age of twenty, Stravinsky's adulthood began.

# Lecture Two
# From Student to Professional

**Scope:** Rimsky-Korsakov, one of the founders of the "Russian Five," began teaching at the St. Petersburg Conservatory in 1871. The composer and his attitudes would exert a lifelong influence on Stravinsky. Stravinsky's first large-scale composition, the Piano Sonata in F Sharp Minor (1904), so impressed Rimsky-Korsakov that he agreed to take Stravinsky on as a private student. In 1906, Stravinsky married his cousin Katya. By 1908, he had established a reputation as a composer of talent. In 1909, Stravinsky met the famous impresario Serge Diaghilev. For the second season of his *Ballets Russes*, Diaghilev planned "the first [real] Russian ballet" and offered the commission—based on the folktale *The Firebird*—to Stravinsky. *The Firebird*, which displays elements of tradition and innovation, was a triumph. During the winter of 1910–11, Stravinsky embarked on "The Great Sacrifice," later known as *The Rite of Spring*. Because the music was not coming to him, he distracted himself by composing the score for the ballet *Petrushka*. Although *Petrushka* was a great success, Stravinsky's next score, *The Rite of Spring*, would become arguably the most influential work of its time.

## Outline

**I.** From 1902 to 1905, Stravinsky became part of Rimsky-Korsakov's inner circle.

   **A.** Stravinsky continued to study music theory and composition with Rimsky-Korsakov's former students.

   **B.** Rimsky-Korsakov was a member of the group known as the "Russian Five."
   1. The others in the group were Cui, Mussorgsky, Borodin, and Balakirev.
   2. They were dedicated to creating a native Russian music based on the operas of Glinka.
   3. They rejected the St. Petersburg and Moscow Conservatories as evidence of foreign influence on Russian art.
   4. "'The Five' made a virtue of their technical ignorance.

- **C.** In 1871, Rimsky-Korsakov tore the group apart by accepting a teaching position at the St. Petersburg Conservatory.
  1. There, as a teacher, he finally mastered the technicalities of music theory and orchestration.
  2. He bridged the musical gap between "The Five" and the European establishment.
  3. He became an influential teacher to Russian composers, such as Stravinsky, Prokofiev, and Glazunov (teacher of Shostakovich).
- **D.** Rimsky-Korsakov was an important and influential man whose attitudes profoundly affected Stravinsky throughout his life.
- **E.** He was so impressed with Stravinsky's first large-scale composition, a four-movement sonata for piano (Piano Sonata in F Sharp Minor, 1904), that he agreed to take him on as a private student in composition and orchestration.
  1. The first movement of this sonata opens with a grand theme. **Musical example:** Piano Sonata in F Sharp Minor, Movement 1.
  2. The second movement is a marvelous and engaging scherzo. **Musical example:** Piano Sonata in F Sharp Minor, Movement 2.

**II.** The other great event of Stravinsky's life was his marriage to his cousin Katya Nosenko in 1906.
- **A.** Because marriage between first cousins was forbidden by law, Stravinsky and Katya were married by "a kind of bootleg priest."
- **B.** Katya gave Stravinsky unqualified support and affection.
  1. She alone recognized that there was something truly exceptional about him and his music.
  2. Without Katya, much of what Stravinsky was about to accomplish would not have been possible.
- **C.** Their first child, Fyodor, was born in February of 1907.

**III.** Stravinsky continued his extraordinary compositional development.
- **A.** He wrote a series of works, including a symphony, that managed to secure him a growing reputation as a composer of talent.
- **B.** He discovered the music of Debussy, which offered him a breath of fresh air that was genuinely seductive.

- **C.** Rimsky-Korsakov's death in 1908, while devastating to Stravinsky, had a liberating effect as well.
- **D.** Stravinsky wrote a brief orchestral work entitled *Fireworks*, which owes more to the French school—in particular Paul Dukas and Claude Debussy—than it does to the Russian. **Musical example:** *Fireworks* (1908), Opening.
- **E.** On January 24, 1909, Stravinsky's *Scherzo Fantastique* was performed at a concert of the Russian Symphony in St. Petersburg. In the audience that night was the impresario Serge Diaghilev.

**IV.** Diaghilev described himself as "a great charlatan."
- **A.** Diaghilev entered university intending to become a lawyer. He soon dropped out and enrolled at the St. Petersburg Conservatory, where he studied composition and dabbled in the arts.
- **B.** Diaghilev's legal training and his interest in art were to be combined in his role as an impresario.
    1. Diaghilev's public importance was his achievement as a manager and a propagandist; his mission was to bring the arts of Russia to the attention of Western Europe in general and Paris in particular.
    2. In 1908, he founded the *Ballets Russes* (Russian Ballet) as a showcase for Russian dancers and designers.
    3. Diaghilev's dance company included great set designers, dancers, and choreographers whose innovative talents changed the whole substance of ballet.
- **C.** Stravinsky orchestrated some Chopin piano works for the inaugural season of the *Ballets Russes* in 1909.
- **D.** For the 1910 season, Diaghilev planned "the first [real] Russian ballet."
- **E.** Diaghilev offered the commission for the ballet score to Stravinsky. The ballet was to be based on the Russian folktale *The Firebird*.
- **F.** Stravinsky turned out the score in just under six months.

**V.** *The Firebird* is a Russian folk tale and an icon in modern Russian society.
- **A.** The story tells of the ogre Kashchey, who holds thirteen princesses as his prisoners. Kashchey's "death" is contained in an egg. If the

egg can be broken in his presence, he will die. With the help of the Firebird, Ivan Tsarevich smashes the egg and frees the princesses.

**B.** Stravinsky's score displays elements of tradition and innovation. Much of the score is written in the style of "The Five." **Musical example:** *The Firebird* (1909), "Khorovode," Finale.

**C.** The celebratory coronation/finale displays aspects of both tradition and innovation. Typical of $19^{th}$-century Russian nationalist music, this finale is based on a preexisting folksong. **Musical example:** *The Firebird*, Finale, Theme.

**D.** Typical of Russian folk music, this finale theme is repeated over and over, seventeen times.
  **1.** Neither the pitches nor the harmony change.
  **2.** The music gets louder and louder as more and more instruments join the celebratory fray.
  **3.** Eventually, it also gets faster.

**E.** What is not typical of $19^{th}$-century Russian nationalist concert music is the way Stravinsky slices and dices this thematic phrase, altering its length and generating musical interest through phrase asymmetry. **Musical example:** *The Firebird*, Finale.

**F.** The most innovative music is the "Infernal Dance of the Ogre Kashchey," in which Stravinsky's use of rhythmic asymmetry creates an extraordinary sense of rhythmic thrust. **Musical example:** *The Firebird*, "Infernal Dance of the Ogre Kashchey," Opening.

**G.** *The Firebird* was a triumph. For the public as well as the press, it was a fully homogenized "Russian ballet product."

**VI.** Stravinsky spent the winter of 1910–11 at Clarens in Switzerland.

**A.** Stravinsky intended to work on "The Great Sacrifice," inspired by a vision he had in which a group of elders watch a young girl dance herself to death as a sacrifice to the god of spring.

**B.** Because the music was not coming to him, he distracted himself by sketching what would become the score for the ballet *Petrushka*. **Musical example:** *Petrushka*, "Russian Dance."
  **1.** Petrushka is a puppet clown.
  **2.** The action of the ballet takes place on two distinct levels: one is human, the other is the world of puppets that come to life.

3. For the rich and varied human environment, Stravinsky needed only to recall the St. Petersburg of his youth. Note the sense of bustle and excitement in this music. **Musical example:** *Petrushka*, Scene I, Opening.
4. The music that Stravinsky wrote for the world of the puppets brilliantly underscores the strangeness of the scene, in which physical reality is twisted into unreality.
5. Stravinsky accomplishes this by presenting two major chords in two different major keys simultaneously (bi-tonality). **Musical example:** *Petrushka*, "Chez Petrushka"—at the piano.
6. This music not only illustrates the strangeness of the scene and Petrushka's jerky motions but also the bipolarity of Petrushka's personality; he is a puppet with the heart of a human. **Musical example:** *Petrushka*, "Chez Petrushka."
7. At this point, Stravinsky's musical style was still a clear outgrowth of Russian nationalism, something that its audiences could understand on their own terms.
8. With choreography by Mikhail Fokine; sets by Alexander Benois; Petruhska and the Ballerina danced by Vaslav Njinsky and Tamara Karsavina, respectively; and the orchestra conducted by Pierre Monteux, *Petrushka* was a phenomenal hit.

**VII.** In 1912, Stravinsky's musical style would change for his creation of *The Rite of Spring*, arguably the most influential work of its time.

# Lecture Three
## *The Rite of Spring*

**Scope:** *The Rite of Spring* changed the way we think about rhythm, melodic patterning, compositional technique, and expressive content. When it opened at the Théâtre des Champs-Elysées in Paris on May 29, 1923, it caused a scandal unparalleled in the history of music. Because the ballet, according to Stravinsky, "is unified by a single idea: the mystery and the great surge of the creative power of the violent Russian spring," he had to conjure up music that sounded like no other, that was primitive, earthy, and sexual. The novelty, and difficulty, of this music was apparent to everyone who heard it. Its lasting modernity is a testament to the fact that it does not sound like any work that preceded it, nor any that followed it. We must know *The Rite* in terms of itself, which is the very essence of modernity. As the virgin danced and died at the end of *The Rite*, a new sort of music and musical aesthetic was born.

## Outline

**I.** What Beethoven's Ninth Symphony was to the 19$^{th}$ century, so Stravinsky's *The Rite of Spring* was to the 20$^{th}$: arguably the most influential work of its time.

   **A.** It changed the way we think about rhythm, melodic patterning, compositional technique, and expressive content.

   **B.** The piece has been used as a metaphor for the breakdown of traditional 19$^{th}$-century values, the new post-Victorian sexuality, and for modernism and the inevitability of the First World War. **Musical example:** *The Rite of Spring* (1912), "The Dance of the Earth," Part 1, Conclusion.

**II.** *The Rite* opened at the Théâtre des Champs-Elysées in Paris on May 29, 1913.

   **A.** A riot broke out among the audience at the premiere. **Musical examples:** *The Rite of Spring*, "Dance of the Adolescents," Opening; "Sacrificial Dance," Opening.

- **B.** Diaghilev had engineered the riot by means of astute advance publicity and ticket distribution. He had even given away seats to "young people" who were instructed to applaud the work at all costs.
- **C.** The brouhaha was as much about the reactions of the audience members to one another as to the work itself.

**III.** *The Rite of Spring* is in two parts.
- **A.** Part One, "The Adoration of the Earth," consists of eight episodes, or *tableaux*, that represent fertility rites, contests, ceremonies, and such.
- **B.** In Part Two, "The Sacrifice," the sacrificial virgin is chosen, glorified, and ultimately danced to death.
- **C.** The theme of *The Rite* is birth and death, primitive and violent, the fundamental experiences of all existence.
    1. To create music that evoked Bronze Age Russia, an environment beyond any particular cultural context, Stravinsky had to conjure up music that sounded like no other, that was primitive, earthy, sexual, and new.
    2. He turned to the two closest elements at hand: his incredible imagination and rhythm.
    3. *The Rite* called for the largest percussion battery ever assembled for a ballet.
    4. The music's heart and soul is drum-like rhythm presented with asymmetrical accentuation.
    5. The "Dance of the Adolescents" is characterized by a single, bi-tonal harmony, carefully constructed so as not to imply any preexisting harmonic reference. This chord (E/E flat) is repeated over and over again in frankly sexual reiterations. Its asymmetrical accentuation *is* the dramatic narrative, the essential discourse. **Musical example:** *The Rite of Spring*, "Dance of the Adolescents," Opening.
    6. Moments later, Stravinsky concludes the episode called "Game of the Abduction" with an incredible, swirling asymmetrical accentuation. **Musical example:** "Game of the Abduction," Conclusion.

- **D.** The lasting modernity of this music, composed nearly one hundred years ago, is a testament to the fact that it does not sound like any work that preceded it, nor any that followed it.
  1. To understand *The Rite*, one must know the work in terms of itself.
  2. That is the essence of modernity.
- **E.** Debussy's influence is apparent throughout the score: in the importance of orchestral *timbre*, the reliance on long-sustained harmonies (pedals) or constantly repeated melodic patterns (*ostinati*), and the use of non-European melodic resources. **Musical example:** *The Rite of Spring*, "Round Dances of Spring" (Archaic Melody).
  1. The opening of *The Rite* resembles a work written by Debussy in 1892. **First musical example:** *The Rite of Spring*, Opening Bassoon Solo; **Second musical example:** Debussy: *Prelude to the Afternoon of a Faun* (1892), Opening Flute Solo.
  2. In his use of *ostinati*, Stravinsky goes far beyond the model of Debussy and uses *ostinati* that overlap each other to create a complex web of rhythmic and melodic patterns. Such a layering of *ostinati* occurs during the "Procession of the Sage." **Musical example:** *The Rite of Spring*, "Procession of the Sage."
- **F.** One of the most original sections of *The Rite* is the introduction.
  1. Here, the earth awakes from its winter's hibernation.
  2. The music does not so much "go anywhere" as simply "accumulate"—it is a wonderful musical metaphor for growth in nature.
  3. When the activity level reaches critical mass, the opening melody returns in the bassoon and the "Dance of the Adolescents" begins. **Musical example:** *The Rite of Spring*, Introduction.
- **G.** Another element of Russian musical tradition that Stravinsky takes to a new level is thematic juxtapositions. **Musical example:** *The Rite of Spring*, "Games of Rival Cities."

**IV.** In October 1912, Stravinsky visited St. Petersburg.
- **A.** Stravinsky's friendships, particularly those with the Rimsky-Korsakov family, had become strained.

- **B.** Members of the St. Petersburg musical community thought Stravinsky had become a Frenchified snob, and they were right.
- **C.** Rimsky-Korsakov's circle believed ballet to be a degenerate art and that Stravinsky had stolen from the dead master in *The Firebird* and *Petrushka*.
- **D.** When Stravinsky left for Switzerland in late October 1912, he would not return to St. Petersburg for fifty years.

**V.** Njinsky's choreography compounded the controversy over *The Rite of Spring*.
- **A.** The choreography, which contains not a single element of traditional ballet, featured a basic position: feet turned inward, knees bent, arms tucked in, and head turned in profile while the body faced forward.
- **B.** These stylized gestures stressed the alienation of modern existence, actually making the dancers part of the composition.

**VI.** The public's interpretation of *The Rite of Spring* as scandalous can be attributed to a number of factors.
- **A.** The theme, basic and at the same time, brutal, lacked moral purpose.
    1. Rebirth, life, and death were depicted without ethical comment.
    2. The only hope was in the energy and fertility of life.
    3. Violent, dissonant, percussive, rhythmically asymmetrical, and cacophonous, the music was as energized and primitive as the theme.
- **B.** But the genius of the work, and its revolutionary impact on Western music, was apparent. In terms of compositional technique and expressive content, *The Rite* was new—a new sort of music and musical aesthetic was born.

# Lecture Four
# The War Years (WWI)

**Scope:** Stravinsky would never compose another work like *The Rite of Spring*, but its techniques would characterize his music until his dying day. The First World War years, a period of consolidation, during which Stravinsky absorbed *The Rite*'s innovation into a less brutal, less dissonant musical language, enforced a certain economy of means on the composer; large-scale works were out of the question. Among the creations of these years were the *Three Pieces for String Quartet* (1914), *Renard* (*The Fox*), for four voices and small orchestra (1916), *Ragtime for Eleven Instruments* (1918), and *L'Histoire du Soldat* (*The Soldier's Tale*) (1918). *Les Noces* (*The Wedding*), begun in 1914 and finished in 1923, is the great masterpiece of this period.

## Outline

**I.** Stravinsky would never compose another work quite like *The Rite of Spring*, but the techniques he honed in that work would characterize his music until his dying day.

    **A.** Following the premiere of *The Rite of Spring*, Stravinsky was occupied with the opera *The Nightingale*. This was Diaghilev's last large-scale production in Paris until after the war.

    **B.** In 1914 in Paris, Pierre Monteux conducted the first performance of the concert version of *Petrushka* and *The Rite of Spring* to popular and critical acclaim.

    **C.** After the birth of their fourth child, Katya suffered a recurrence of childhood tuberculosis.

    **D.** Katya's illness and the outbreak of war in August 1914 forced the Stravinskys to remain in Switzerland.

**II.** Compositionally, the years of World War I were a period of consolidation for Stravinsky.

    **A.** Stravinsky absorbed the innovations of *The Rite* into a less brutal, less dissonant musical language.

        **1.** The war forced a certain economy of means on Stravinsky. Large-scale works were out of the question.

    **2.** Among the creations of the war years were *Three Pieces for String Quartet* (1914); *Renard* (*The Fox*) for four voices and small orchestra (1916); *Les Noces* (*The Wedding*), the great masterpiece of these years (1917); *Ragtime for Eleven Instruments* (1918); and *L'Histoire du Soldat* (*The Soldier's Tale*) (1918).

**B.** *Three Pieces for String Quartet* is an example of post-*Rite* miniaturization, demonstrating, as it does, all the compositional techniques of *The Rite* in the context of a string quartet. **Musical example:** *Three Pieces for String Quartet,* No. 1.
    **1.** Each instrument has its own music. **Musical examples:** first violin part, second violin part, viola part, cello part—at the piano.
    **2.** This music is about time and our perception of time, about shifting instrumental relationships and juxtapositions, about phase and focus. This is conceptual art in which the execution of the concept—the actual music—is as interesting as the concept itself. **Musical example:** *Three Pieces for String Quartet*, No. 1.

**C.** In July 1914, Stravinsky made a quick visit to Russia.
    **1.** This would be his last visit to Russia until 1962.
    **2.** He returned to Switzerland with collections of folk poetry and songs and books on language that were to provide the inspiration for the great bulk of his music through 1920.
    **3.** Stravinsky wrote his own libretto for *Renard*, basing it on a Russian folktale.
    **4.** *Renard* is scored for four singers (two tenors and two basses) and a small orchestra.
    **5.** Completed in 1916, *Renard* was not performed until 1922.
    **6.** Stravinsky insisted that the libretto (originally in Russian) be sung in the language of its audience.
    **7.** The story of *Renard* involves a rooster, who brags about his harem of hens, and a wily fox, who is outwitted and ultimately destroyed by farmyard animals. **Musical examples:** *Renard*, Instrumental Introduction; Rooster's Opening Lines; "The Death of Renard."

**D.** With *Ragtime for Eleven Instruments* (1918), Stravinsky wanted to create a sort of composite portrait of what he called "new North American dance music."
   **1.** What Stravinsky knew as "ragtime" was the "bleached" version popularized by the music publishing industry based in New York, music that drew on the rhythmic elements of genuine ragtime but watered them down for a primarily white audience.
   **2.** The quintessential example of such popularized ragtime was Irving Berlin's *Alexander's Ragtime Band*. **Musical example:** Berlin, *Alexander's Ragtime Band*.
   **3.** Ask yourself whether this music sounds like ragtime, "bleached" or "unbleached." **Musical example:** *Ragtime for Eleven Instruments*, Opening.
   **4.** This music is assuredly not ragtime in any form.
   **5.** It is a quirky, witty instrumental work, an almost Cubist version of ragtime-like music, in which the elements have all been rearranged, unexpectedly juxtaposed, and de-contextualized.
   **6.** *Ragtime for Eleven Instruments* is music about music and, compositionally, it is pure, post-*Rite of Spring* Stravinsky. **Musical example:** *Ragtime for Eleven Instruments*, Opening.

**E.** *Les Noces* (*The Wedding*) brings together Russian folklore, as well as all the compositional techniques that we have observed thus far.
   **1.** Stravinsky first thought of writing a "dance cantata" on the subject of a Russian peasant wedding in 1912, while at work on *The Rite of Spring*.
   **2.** In 1914, the piece began to take genuine shape.
   **3.** Stravinsky assembled the text, which represents a "wedding day slice of life," from a collection of Russian popular poems and songs.
   **4.** *The Wedding* has four scenes and calls for a four-part chorus and four vocal soloists.
   **5.** The work is scored for four pianos, timpani, bells, xylophones, and various drums.
   **6.** *The Wedding* is ritual music about ritual; the music is stripped of all expressive nuance and embellishment.
   **7.** The first scene is a lament sung by the bride and her bridesmaids; the bride's hair is a symbol of her youth,

innocence, and virginity, all soon to be lost. **Musical example:** *The Wedding* (1917), First Tableau, Opening.
8. The second scene takes place at the bridegroom's house.
9. The third scene marks the departure of the bride from the house of her parents.
10. The fourth scene is entitled "The Red Table," or sometimes "The Wedding Feast." A brilliant, comic, and touching episode that sees the wedding ceremony, the meeting of the two families, the wedding toasts, the feast, the preparation of the wedding bed, and finally, the bride and groom contemplating their life together. This fourth scene opens with a celebratory poem that is a metaphor for the joining of the bride and groom. **Musical example:** *The Wedding*, Fourth Tableau, Opening.
11. *The Wedding* ends quietly and quite beautifully with the tolling of the wedding bells as the chorus sings.

# Lecture Five
# Neoclassicism

**Scope:** In 1919, Diaghilev proposed a ballet based on music by the Italian baroque composer Pergolesi. Immediately after the war, many felt a nostalgic hearkening back to seemingly more humane times. Diaghilev sensed these currents and, in fact, had not lost a bit of his impresario's acumen. For Stravinsky, the new ballet—*Pulcinella*—was an opportunity to discover the past. Although some of the melodies might be by Pergolesi, other compositional components are pure Stravinsky. In 1921, Stravinsky attended a cabaret in Paris, where he met Sergey Sudeykin and his wife, Vera, with whom he would fall passionately in love. Their subsequent affair continued until Katya's death in 1938, which opened the way for their marriage. From 1920 to 1923, Stravinsky composed the *Symphonies for Wind Instruments*, the opera *Mavra*, the Octet for Wind Instruments, the Concerto for Piano and Wind Instruments, and the four-piano version of *The Wedding*.

## Outline

I. The war and the Russian Revolution had tragic consequences for Stravinsky.
   - **A.** Stravinsky's brother Gury died of typhoid fever while serving in the Russian army.
   - **B.** His family's summer home in Ustilug suffered substantial damage.
   - **C.** The Russian Revolution and its aftermath left Stravinsky depressed and virtually destitute.

II. Because of the Revolution and the copyright laws of the day, Stravinsky's most popular work, *The Firebird*, was already in the public domain.
   - **A.** After 1917, Stravinsky received nothing from performances of *The Firebird*.
   - **B.** He hit on the idea of making a suite out of the ballet.
      1. Such an arrangement could be published as a new work.

2. So emerged Stravinsky's lifelong habit of re-orchestrating his most popular works every 28 years to ensure that he would keep some rights to them.

**III.** By 1917, Diaghilev and his *Ballets Russes* were close to bankruptcy.
 **A.** Diaghilev decided that because *Petrushka* was published in Germany and *The Firebird*, in Russia, he was not legally obligated to pay Stravinsky for their use.
 **B.** This infuriated Stravinsky, but despite the bitterness, these two men could not be kept apart by money.

**IV.** In 1919, Diaghilev proposed an idea for a new project that would become *Pulcinella*.
 **A.** Stravinsky later wrote that he thought Diaghilev was insane to propose Pergolesi, but he "fell in love" with the $18^{th}$-century composer when he looked at the music.
 **B.** Why would Diaghilev choose, as his first major post-war production, a ballet based on music by an obscure Italian baroque composer? Diaghilev, in fact, had not lost a bit of his acumen.
  1. In 1919, Europe was emerging from a long and terrible nightmare.
  2. In the years following the war, many felt a hearkening back to seemingly "better," more humane times.
  3. Diaghilev sensed these currents as well as anyone.
 **C.** Of his own attraction, Stravinsky wrote that "*Pulcinella* was my discovery of the past."
 **D.** While some of the melodies might be by Pergolesi, many elements are pure Stravinsky, $20^{th}$-century composer, $20^{th}$-century man. These elements include:
  1. Harmonic usage
  2. Instrumentation
  3. Treatment of phrase structure
  4. Asymmetrical rhythmic elements
  5. Juxtapositions
  6. Patterning, and so forth.
  7. **Musical example:** *Pulcinella* (1919), Overture/Sinfonia.

- **E.** The second movement, "Serenade," is so lyric and beautifully scored that on first listening, we might not notice that the harmony is entirely static—it does not go anywhere. **Musical example:** *Pulcinella*, "Serenade."
- **F.** Familiar 18$^{th}$-century musical "objects" are not being used in an 18$^{th}$-century sense. The melodies do not develop, the harmonies do not progress, the rhythmic groupings do not stay symmetrical.
    1. This is art about art.
    2. *Pulcinella* is not arranged and orchestrated Pergolesi; it is pure Stravinsky.
- **G.** The fourth movement, "Tarantella," is a very fast Neapolitan dance. **Musical example:** *Pulcinella*, "Tarantella."
- **H.** The seventh movement, "Vivo," is pure comic burlesque. **Musical example:** *Pulcinella*, "Vivo."
- **I.** The finale is brilliant; it features all those elements we have noted to this point, all delivered via a rhythmic thrust and energy that is much more typical of the 20$^{th}$ century than the 18$^{th}$ century. **Musical example:** *Pulcinella*, Finale.
- **J.** *Pulcinella* was premiered in Paris on May 15, 1920. The choreographer, Leonid Massine, danced the title role. Tamara Karsavina was Pimpinella. Pablo Picasso designed the sets, and Ernest Ansermet conducted.

**V.** On February 19, 1921, Stravinsky, Diaghilev, the designer Sergey Sudeykin, and his wife, Vera, attended a Russian-style cabaret show in Paris.
- **A.** Vera, painter, costume designer, and former actress, had helped make the costumes for the show.
- **B.** Five months later, Stravinsky fell head over heels in love with her.
- **C.** What began as a passionate love affair became, for Stravinsky and Vera, a double life, until Katya's death in 1938.
- **D.** Stravinsky and Vera were finally married in March of 1940.

**VI.** From 1920 to 1923, Stravinsky continued to compose a series of superb works, including *Symphonies for Wind Instruments*, the opera *Mavra*, Octet for Wind Instruments, the Concerto for Piano and Wind Instruments, and the final, four-piano version of *The Wedding*.

**A.** In May of 1922, Vera left her husband.
**B.** By this time, Stravinsky had also told Katya about his affair.
**C.** At the same time, Stravinsky's mother, Anna, with whom he did not have the best relationship, paid a visit.

# Lecture Six
# Maturity

**Scope:** By the mid-1920s, Stravinsky's musical philosophy embraced the belief that a composition should be governed by purely formal considerations—it should not have a literary or pictorial interest. He found a purity and precision in 18th-century music that was the antithesis of Romanticism. He spent the first ten weeks of 1924 performing and conducting in the United States. During the late 1920s, he produced the opera-oratorio *Oedipus Rex* (1927), the ballet *Apollo* (1928), *The Fairy's Kiss* (1928), the *Capriccio* for Piano and Orchestra (1929), and *The Symphony of Psalms* (1930). Each of these works filters its modernism through the lens of the musical past. Commissioned by the Boston Symphony, *The Symphony of Psalms* is a deeply religious work, the sort Stravinsky had never written before. The same elements in *The Rite of Spring* are present in *The Symphony of Psalms*. What *is* different is the austerity of *The Symphony of Psalms*.

## Outline

I. In 1923, Stravinsky wrote that each of his works is a "musical object."

   A. He went on to explain that a composition is governed by purely formal considerations, in which all expressive nuance has been ruthlessly excluded in favor of motoric melodies and strict tempo relationships that articulate the essential compositional process—counterpoint.

   B. He also claimed that music itself can have no literary or pictorial interest.

   C. This philosophy is demonstrated in the works of the mid-1920s: The Octet for Winds (1923), the Concerto for Piano and Wind Instruments (1924), and the Piano Sonata (1925).

II. Stravinsky's Piano Sonata of 1925 is in three movements.

   A. The Piano Sonata is evocative of Bach in terms of its linear clarity, its overwhelming emphasis on counterpoint, and the brittle, almost harpsichord-like tone Stravinsky demands from the piano.

- **B.** During the first movement, the pianist's hands are often playing in two entirely different keys. This is very "modern" music. **Musical example:** Piano Sonata, Movement 1.
- **C.** The *Adagietto* is more evocative of Beethoven than Bach, as shown in the following comparison. **Musical examples:** Beethoven, Piano Sonata in F Minor, Op. 2, No. 1; Stravinsky, Piano Sonata, Movement 2, Opening.
- **D.** Resemblances aside, Stravinsky's work has a modernity and frank artificiality that mark it as light years away from Beethoven's.
- **E.** The third movement again recalls, on its surface only, the music of Bach. **Musical example:** Piano Sonata, Movement 3.

**III.** Stravinsky never stopped being a true modern.
- **A.** What he found in the music of the 18th century was an aesthetic purity and compositional precision that was the antithesis of Romanticism.
- **B.** Stravinsky's *Rite* is like a kaleidoscope: in any given episode (tableau), the individual materials do not change; what changes constantly is the relationship between the materials. **Musical example:** *The Rite of Spring*, "Adoration of the Earth," Finale, Part I.
- **C.** Stravinsky's views were deeply influenced by Jacques Maritain's *Art et Scholastique* (1920), which gave meaning to Stravinsky's feelings about his own art and life.

**IV.** Stravinsky visited the United States in 1925.
- **A.** He spent the first ten weeks of 1925 performing and conducting his music in several cities in America, including New York, Boston, Chicago, Philadelphia, Cleveland, and Cincinnati. **Musical example:** Concerto for Piano and Wind Instruments, Movement 3, Opening.
- **B.** Stravinsky later told European reporters he was inspired by America's "gigantic growth" and the fact that "everyone works."
- **C.** America loved Stravinsky, too. After a ten-week tour, he returned to Europe with $25,000, the equivalent of over a half million dollars today.

**V.** During the late 1920s, Stravinsky produced the opera-oratorio *Oedipus Rex*, libretto in Latin by Jean Cocteau (1927); the ballet *Apollo* (1928); *The Fairy's Kiss*, inspired by the music of Tchaikovsky (1928); the *Capriccio* for Piano and Orchestra (1929); and *The Symphony of Psalms* (1930).

   **A.** Each of these works filters its modernism through the lens of the musical past. **Musical example:** *Apollo Musagète*, "The Birth of Apollo," Opening.

   **B.** The quiet and elegant *Apollo*, Stravinsky's first ballet in eight years, would seem to have completely done away with everything that had once been typically "Stravinskyan."

**VI.** *The Symphony of Psalms* (1930) is a deeply religious work, the sort of music Stravinsky had never written before.

   **A.** Events had conspired to bring about his religious rebirth.
   1. Stravinsky was born into the Russian Orthodox Church.
   2. Although never a practicing Christian, he had religion in his blood.
   3. In July of 1928, Diaghilev died in Venice.
   4. Robert Craft theorizes that Stravinsky's guilt over his affair with Vera pushed him toward religion.
   5. In exile from his beloved Russia, Stravinsky sought the solace of the church.

   **B.** In 1930, Stravinsky was offered a commission of $6000 (about $125,000 today) from the Boston Symphony Orchestra in celebration of its fiftieth anniversary season; he composed *The Symphony of Psalms*.
   1. The same compositional elements in *The Rite of Spring* are present in *The Symphony of Psalms*.
   2. What *is* different is the austerity of *The Symphony of Psalms*, which shares its magnificence with Bach's B Minor Mass and St. Matthew Passion, Beethoven's *Missa Solemnis*, and Verdi's Requiem.
   3. Stravinsky's *Symphony of Psalms* is in three movements.
   4. The texts are drawn from the vulgate Latin version of the Psalms.
   5. The piece begins with a series of E minor chords that telescope outward. **Musical example:** *The Symphony of Psalms*, Movement 1, Instrumental Opening.

6. The brilliant second movement is a double fugue. The opening becomes a metaphor for the loneliness of the individual. The slow but inevitable entrance of more and more instrumental voices becomes a metaphor for the multitude raising their voices to God. The polyphony created by the voice entries is a metaphor for the wilderness invoked by the text. **Musical examples:** *The Symphony of Psalms*, Movement 2, Fugue Subject (in oboe only).
7. This extraordinary fugue subject is itself nothing but an expansion and elongation of the minor-third *ostinato* of the first movement.
8. The introductory fugue represents a polyphonic "wilderness." **Musical example:** Wind Fugue, Opening (four voice entries).
9. The third movement opens with a passage built over an *ostinato* that slowly outlines a C major chord. **Musical example:** *Symphony of Psalms*, Movement 3 ("Chariot of Elijah"), Opening.
10. *The Symphony of Psalms* reaches its climax in a magnificent passage. The music seems to float, unhindered by any tonal or rhythmic gravity. **Musical example:** *The Symphony of Psalms*, Movement 3, Closing *ostinato*.
11. The economy of means in *The Symphony of Psalms* is remarkable, even by Stravinsky's standards.

# Lecture Seven
## A Citizen of the World

**Scope:** With the outbreak of World War II, Stravinsky and Vera left for the United States. They were married on March 9, 1940. The Stravinskys soon afterward settled in the Los Angeles area, where Stravinsky instantly became one of Hollywood's most sought-after celebrities. Stravinsky's first major work composed entirely in the United States was the *Symphony in Three Movements*, the "War Symphony." Among the works Stravinsky wrote in these years were the *Ebony* Concerto (1945), the Concerto in D for String Orchestra (1946), the ballet *Orpheus* (1947), the Mass (1948), the opera *The Rake's Progress* (1951), and the Septet (1953). In 1948, Stravinsky met Robert Craft, then twenty-four years old, and offered him a job. Thus began a relationship unique in the history of music. Craft exposed the composer to twelve-tone music. Stravinsky, in his early seventies, was about to change his compositional language—substantially—and in doing so, enter an entirely new musical world.

## Outline

**I.** In 1934, Stravinsky became a French citizen. Life in Russia (under Stalin) or Germany (under Hitler) was becoming increasingly out of the question.

**II.** Among Stravinsky's great works of the 1930s were the Concerto in D for Violin (1931), *Persephone* (1934), the Concerto for Two Pianos (1935), the ballet *A Card Game* (1936), and the Concerto in E Flat Major (*Dumbarton Oaks*) (1938).

    **A.** These works exhibit the sort of neoclassical, or neotonal, stylistic language we have already observed in *Pulcinella,* the Piano Sonata, and *The Symphony of Psalms*.

    **B.** The Concerto in D for Violin was written for virtuoso and friend Samuel Dushkin.

1. It is brilliant, lyric, and perfectly suited for the violin. **Musical example:** Concerto in D for Violin, Movement 1, Opening.
2. The chord D–E–A, in a different dress, begins each one of the four movements. **Musical examples:** Concerto in D for Violin, Opening Chord from Movements 1, 2, 3, 4.

C. The Concerto for Two Pianos (1935) was originally written for performance by Stravinsky and his son Soulima.
1. This work is much more a sonata for two pianos than a true concerto.
2. The pianos are blended together to create a megapiano, rather than performing as solo instruments in the style of a traditional concerto. **Musical examples:** Concerto for Two Pianos, Movement 1, Opening; Concerto for Two Pianos, Movement 2 (*Notturno*: *Adagietto*), Opening.

D. The *Dumbarton Oaks* Concerto was commissioned in 1937 from Mr. and Mrs. Robert Woods Bliss of Washington, D.C.
1. The concerto was premiered in Washington, D.C., in May of 1938, under the baton of Nadia Boulanger.
2. Stravinsky described the works as "A little concerto in the style of [Bach's] *Brandenburg* Concertos." **Musical example:** J. S. Bach, *Brandenburg* Concerto No. 2, Movement 3, Opening.
3. Stravinsky's concerto is scored for a Bach-sized ensemble of fifteen instruments, all of which are treated, at some point or another, as solo instruments. **Musical example:** *Dumbarton Oaks* Concerto, Movement 1 (*Tempo giusto*).

III. The years 1938 to 1939 would prove memorable in Stravinsky's life.

A. First came another commission from Mr. and Mrs. Robert Woods Bliss for a symphonic work to celebrate the fiftieth anniversary of the Chicago Symphony (eventually to become the *Symphony in C*).

B. Stravinsky was invited by Harvard University to speak in association with the Charles Eliot Norton Chair.

C. Stravinsky's music was attacked at the Nazi-sponsored exhibition of "Degenerate Art" in Dusseldorf.

- **D.** Personal tragedy also struck. Stravinsky's daughter, Lyudmilla, his wife, Katya, and his mother all died within seven months of one another.
- **E.** Stravinsky checked himself into the Sancellemoz sanitarium, where he continued work on the *Symphony in C* and his Norton lectures. **Musical example:** *Symphony in C*, Movement 1, Opening.

**IV.** Stravinsky and Vera emigrated to the United States in 1939.
- **A.** On September 1, 1939, World War II began. Stravinsky and Vera Sudeykin boarded a ship bound for the United States.
- **B.** They arrived on September 30$^{th}$.
- **C.** The Norton Lectures were delivered at Harvard.
- **D.** Concerts of Stravinsky's music took place in New York.
- **E.** Stravinsky married Vera on March 9, 1940.
- **F.** He and Vera settled in the Los Angeles area in the fall of 1940.
    1. Stravinsky completed the *Symphony in C*.
    2. In November 1940, the Stravinskys bought a house in Hollywood, where they would live for twenty-nine years, until Stravinsky's final illness forced a move to New York.
    3. Stravinsky instantly became one of Hollywood's most sought-after celebrities.
- **G.** *Symphony in Three Movements*, the "War Symphony," was Stravinsky's first major work composed in the United States.
    1. The opening and closing movements display an unusual level of violence and fury. **Musical example:** *Symphony in Three Movements* (1945), Movement 1.
    2. *Symphony in Three Movements* is vintage Stravinsky with a veneer of violence reminiscent of *The Rite of Spring*.
    3. The third and final movement of the *Symphony in Three Movements* is more like *The Rite of Spring* than anything Stravinsky had written in years. But it ends with a chord that sounds like pure Hollywood/big-band jazz. **Musical example:** *Symphony in Three Movements*, Movement 3.
    4. Stravinsky finished the *Symphony in Three Movements* in August 1945.
- **H.** On December 28, 1945, the Stravinskys became U.S. citizens.

**V.** The years following the war were the best of Stravinsky's life.
   **A.** He was happily married.
   **B.** His health flourished.
   **C.** Financial woes were a thing of the past.
   **D.** He was never lonely for companionship, because the United States had become the haven and home for countless uprooted European artists and intellectuals.
   **E.** Among the works Stravinsky wrote in these years were the *Ebony* Concerto (1945), the Concerto in D for String Orchestra (1946), the ballet *Orpheus* (1947), the Mass (1948), the opera *The Rake's Progress* (1951), and the Septet (1953).

**VI.** In 1948, Stravinsky met Robert Craft.
   **A.** Craft was a twenty-four-year-old Juilliard graduate, a fledgling conductor, and a huge Stravinsky fanatic.
   **B.** Craft kept a diary during his more than twenty years with Stravinsky.
   **C.** Stravinsky took to Craft right away and offered him a job as his assistant.
      **1.** Thus began a relationship unique in the history of music.
      **2.** Craft was quickly enlisted to help with the prosody of the opera *The Rake's Progress*, which was being set in English, a language with which Stravinsky was not yet completely comfortable.
   **D.** Craft exposed the composer to the twelve-tone music of Schoenberg, Berg, and Webern.
      **1.** Stravinsky, in his early seventies, was about to change his compositional language for the first time in over thirty years.
      **2.** In doing so, he would enter an entirely new musical world.

**VII.** In 1945, Stravinsky, taken with Woody Herman's recordings, decided to write a piece for the band.
   **A.** The *Ebony* Concerto was premiered by Woody Herman's band on March 25, 1946, at Carnegie Hall.
   **B.** The piece drove the critics crazy. Was it jazz? **Musical Example:** *Ebony* Concerto, Movement 1, Opening.

**C.** Just as he had done in his *Ragtime for Eleven Instruments*, Stravinsky objectifies big-band jazz by cutting, pasting, and juxtaposing its original elements to create a kaleidoscopic, almost Cubist work.

**D.** The *Ebony* Concerto, like *Ragtime for Eleven Instruments*, *Pulcinella*, and so much of Stravinsky's other post-1920/pre-1950 music, is music about music. **Musical example:** *Ebony* Concerto, Movement 3, Conclusion.

# Lecture Eight
# The New Stravinsky

**Scope:** The parallels between Schoenberg and Stravinsky are many. The great masterwork of Schoenberg's so-called "freely atonal music" is *Pierrot Lunaire*. Along with *The Rite of Spring*, *Pierrot Lunaire* is the most important musical composition of the 20th century. In the early 1950s, Robert Craft began conducting serial works by Schoenberg and his students Alban Berg and Anton Webern. Not surprisingly, this music captured Stravinsky's interest. Serial music is highly intellectualized and formulaic, which is exactly what Stravinsky's music had been all about from almost the beginning of his compositional career. In 1962, Stravinsky visited Russia for the first time since 1914. The tour was a huge success, as well as an emotionally charged experience. Stravinsky's late works, like Beethoven's late works, attain a level of spirituality, clarity, and novelty almost unique in the repertoire. *Requiem Canticles* (1966), Stravinsky's last major work, is considered the most accessible of his late works. In 1969, for medical reasons, Stravinsky and his entourage moved to New York City. He died on April 6, 1971, and was buried in Venice on the island of San Michele.

## Outline

I. The parallels between Schoenberg and Stravinsky are many.
   **A.** Both Stravinsky and Schoenberg were essentially self-taught.
   **B.** Their imaginations were never squelched by having learned to do things the "right way."
   **C.** Both composers grew up in extraordinarily rich cultural and musical environments.
      **1.** For Stravinsky, the environment was St. Petersburg.
      **2.** For Schoenberg, it was the imperial city of Vienna.

II. Schoenberg believed in all those compositional and expressive elements that 19th-century German and Austrian composers believed in.

- A. What Arnold Schoenberg did not believe in was the traditional harmonic language and the sorts of melodies that sprang forth from that harmonic language.
- B. He began writing a freely melodic music—erroneously called "atonal"—in which the vertical, or harmonic, aspect of the music was determined entirely by the interplay of melody, rather than the other way around.
    1. The great masterwork of Schoenberg's so-called "freely atonal music" is *Pierrot Lunaire*.
    2. Along with *The Rite of Spring*, *Pierrot Lunaire* is the most important musical composition of the 20$^{th}$ century. **Musical example:** *Pierrot Lunaire*, "Moondrunk."

III. Fundamentally, Stravinsky and Schoenberg admired each other's music, although as their careers advanced and their music developed, each composer was increasingly critical of the other.
- A. Ultimately, they both landed in Los Angeles, where for eleven years, they were virtually neighbors.
- B. During that time, they never once met each other.

IV. In the early 1950s, Robert Craft began conducting works by Schoenberg and his students Alban Berg and Anton Webern in Los Angeles.
- A. Stravinsky was fascinated by the so-called "twelve-tone" music of Schoenberg and Webern.
- B. For Stravinsky—master musical objectivist that he was—this growing fascination was a logical progression from his "objectivist" neoclassical/neotonal music.
- C. At the age of seventy, Stravinsky's music underwent a tremendous aesthetic metamorphosis.
- D. The musical world considered Stravinsky's embrace of so-called "Viennese serialists" to be heresy and sacrilege.

V. "Serial" music (and Stravinsky's late music) was a highly intellectualized, formulaic music.
- A. It broke entirely with the emotional *angst* and expression of Romanticism and nationalism.
- B. This is exactly what Stravinsky's music had been all about:

1. Objectivity
2. The use of compositional processes, such as layering and juxtaposing
3. Complete avoidance of the extra-musical references and emotionalism of Romanticism.

C. In retrospect, Stravinsky's turn to the modernism of serialism would seem a historical inevitability.

D. Stravinsky's late music consists of the Septet (1953), *In Memoriam Dylan Thomas* (1954), *Canticum Sacrum* (1955), the ballet *Agon* (1957), *Threni* (1958), and *Movements* for piano and orchestra (1959).

VI. *Agon* was composed from 1953 to 1957.

A. *Agon* contains elements of both Stravinsky's "old," neoclassic/neotonal, compositional style and his "new" serial style.

B. The opening fanfare was the first music written for *Agon* in 1953. It is "old style" Stravinsky: crisp, brilliant, neotonal, and in comparison with what is to come, quite accessible. **Musical example:** *Agon*, Opening Fanfare, "Pas-de-Quatre."

C. *Agon* consists of twenty-one different dance episodes, some of them neotonal in style and some, serial. **Musical example:** *Agon*, "Pas-de-Deux," Opening.

VII. Stravinsky's last years were good and active years, both privately and professionally.

A. No tour was more important for Stravinsky than the one he made with Vera and Craft to Russia in 1962, in celebration of his eightieth birthday.
1. Stravinsky had not been in Russia since 1914.
2. He visited Moscow and Leningrad (St. Petersburg), where both he and Craft conducted his works.
3. In Leningrad, they met a nephew of Diaghilev and Rimsky-Korsakov's son Vladimir, experiences that reduced both men to tears.

B. Craft has described Stravinsky as following a strict routine in his work habits. Craft did not believe Stravinsky ever separated himself from work, even when he was "physically absent from it."

- **C.** Stravinsky's private life included going to movies and listening to records, especially, in his last years, recordings of Beethoven's late string quartets. He also played Chinese checkers and Scrabble with Vera, and received visits from his friends, who included Aldous Huxley, Christopher Isherwood, and Gerald Heard.
- **D.** He had attained celebrity and wealth rarely accorded a composer.
- **E.** He was surrounded by people who loved him.
- **F.** Like Beethoven's late works, Stravinsky's attain a level of spirituality, clarity and novelty.
- **G.** Most of these works are liturgical: *Canticum Sacrum* (1956); *Threni* (1957); *A Sermon, Narrative and a Prayer* (1961); *The Flood* (1962); *Abraham and Isaac* (1963); *Introitus* (1965); and *Requiem Canticles* (1966).

**VIII.** *Requiem Canticles* (1966) was Stravinsky's last major work.
- **A.** Stravinsky extracted the texts from the Catholic Requiem Mass (Mass for the Dead).
- **B.** The significance of an elderly composer setting portions of the Mass for the Dead is impossible for us to escape.
- **C.** It is generally considered the most accessible of Stravinsky's late works.
- **D.** This brief piece has nine sections.
- **E.** The work opens with a buzzing, almost insect-like Prelude for strings. **Musical example:** *Requiem Canticles*, Prelude.
- **F.** The second movement is prayerful and exquisite, in which the gathered multitude or host implores God "Oh, Hear My Prayer." **Musical example:** *Requiem Canticles*, "Exaudi."
- **G.** The fourth movement, "Tuba Mirum," is scored for solo baritone, brass, and bassoons. **Musical example:** *Requiem Canticles*, "Tuba Mirum."
- **H.** The fifth and middle movement is scored for flutes, bassoons, horns, and timpani. Notice the ethereal repeated chord that acts as a thematic refrain in this interlude. In terms of its compositional function, this magical harmony and its asymmetrical repetitions serve the same purpose and play the same role as the brutal E/E flat chord from "Dance of the Adolescents," written fifty-four years before. **Musical example:** *Requiem Canticles*, Interlude.

**IX.** Stravinsky made his last public appearance in 1967.
  **A.** From 1967 on, Stravinsky's health began to fail.
  **B.** For medical reasons, he and his entourage moved to New York City in 1969.
  **C.** He died in his apartment on Fifth Avenue on April 6, 1971.
  **D.** His wife and friends decided that Stravinsky, a Russian by birth and an American citizen for thirty years, would be buried in Venice, his favorite city, in the Orthodox cemetery on the island of San Michele, a few steps away from the grave of Serge Diaghilev.
  **E.** Vera, who died in 1983 at the age of ninety-four, was buried beside her husband.

# Vocal Texts

## Stravinsky: *The Wedding* (*Los Noces*)
### Scene 1 ("The Tresses")

**The Bride**
Tress my tress, O thou fair tress of my hair,
O my little tress.
My mother brushed thee, mother brushed thee at evening,
Mother brushed my tress.
O woe is me, O alas poor me.

**Bridesmaids**
I comb her tresses, her fair golden tresses,
Nastasia's bright hair, Timofeevna's fair tresses.
I comb and plait it, with ribbon red I twine it,
I will twine her golden hair.
I comb her fair tresses, bright golden tresses,
I comb and twine Timofeevna's fair tresses,
I bind her tresses, I comb them and plait them,
With a fine comb I dress them.

**The Bride**
Cruel, heartless came the matchmaker,
Pitiless, cruel, pitiless cruel one, pitiless cruel one,
She tore my tresses, tore my bright golden hair, pulled it, tearing it,
She tore my hair that she might plait it in
Two plaits, plaiting it in two.
O woe is me, woe is me.

### Scene 4 ("The Red Table" or "The Wedding Feast")
**Opening Celebratory Poem**
There were two berries on a branch, they fell to the ground,
One berry bows to the other berry.
Ai, louli, louli, louli! Louchenki, ai louli,
A red, a very red one, and a strawberry did ripen,
Ai Louchenki, louli.
And one berry spoke sweetly to the other,
Close one berry grew to the other,
And one berry represents the noble bridegroom, Fetis,
And the other, the white one, 'tis Nastasia.

# Stravinsky: *Renard*

**Rooster (opening lines)**
Chuck, chuck, chuck, chuck, chuck, chuck-a-dah, chuck-a-dah,
I'm the king of my yard, chuck-a-day.
I with my spurs will cut him.
I with my knife will cut him.
Beat him black and blue,
Then stick a knife in him too.

Chuck, chuck, chuck, chuck, chuck, chuck-a-dah, chuck-a-dah,
Oh bring him to me quickly.
You'll be too late.
Don't wait, you'll be too late.

Chuck, chuck, chuck, chuck, chuck, chuck-a-dah, chuck-a-dah,
Now the knife is ready;
It's a very sharp knife.
Say good-bye to your life.
He'll get such a banging,
Then there'll be a hanging.

Chuck, chuck, chuck, chuck, chuck, chuck-a-dah, chuck-a-dah,
For the knife is ready waiting
And the rope is oscillating.
He'll get such a banging, banging,
Followed by a hanging, hanging.

**Renard** (*disguised as a nun*)
**(opening lines)**
Greetings, my little red-head beauty.
Put aside your pride and come down, sir.
Tell me all your sins.

## Death of Renard

**Renard** (*talking to his tail*)
You scoundrel!
Let the beasts tear you to bits!
**Chorus**
Brother Fox, dear Foxy,
Why did you have to leave us?

'Cos I've work to do at home.
I must do it all alone.

## **Schoenberg: *Pierrot Lunaire***
### "Moondrunk"

The wine that only eyes may drink
Pours from the moon in waves at nightfall
And like a spring flood overwhelms
The still horizon rim.
Desires, shivering and sweet,
Are swimming without number through the
Flood waters!
The wine that only eyes may drink
Pours from the moon in waves at nightfall.
The poet, by his ardor driven,
Grown drunken with the holy drink
To heaven he rapturously lifts
His head and reeling sips and swallows
The wine that only eyes may drink.

# Timeline

| | |
|---|---|
| 1882 | Born in Oranienbaum, Russia, June 17. |
| 1899 | Begins piano lessons with Leokadiya Kashperova. |
| 1901 | Enters University of St. Petersburg's Law School. |
| 1904 | Becomes student of Nicolai Rimski-Korsakov. |
| 1906 | Marries Katya Nosenko. |
| 1909 | Meets Serge Diaghilev; *Firebird*. |
| 1911 | *Petrushka*. |
| 1912 | Leaves St. Petersburg for Switzerland. |
| 1913 | *The Rite of Spring* premieres in Paris. |
| 1914 | World War I begins. |
| 1917 | Russian Revolution begins; *The Wedding* (*Les Noces*). |
| 1920 | *Pulcinella* premieres in Paris. |
| 1921 | Stravinsky meets Vera Sudeykin. |
| 1925 | Tours U.S.; Piano Sonata. |
| 1928 | Diaghilev dies in Venice; *Apollo*. |
| 1930 | *Symphony of Psalms*. |
| 1931 | Violin Concerto in D Major. |
| 1934 | Stravinsky becomes a French citizen. |
| 1938 | *Dumbarton Oaks* Concerto premieres in Washington, D.C. |
| 1939 | Stravinsky's mother and wife, Katya, die; World War II begins; goes to U.S. |

|      | to give Norton Lectures at Harvard University. |
|------|------|
| 1940 | Marries Vera Sudeykin; *Symphony in C*; moves to Hollywood. |
| 1945 | *Symphony in Three Movements*; becomes a U.S. citizen. |
| 1948 | Robert Craft enters Stravinsky's life. |
| 1957 | *Agon.* |
| 1962 | Stravinsky tours Russia. |
| 1966 | *Requiem Canticles* premieres in Princeton, NJ. |
| 1971 | Dies in New York on April 6. |

# Glossary

**atonality**: The absence of an established tonality, or identifiable key.

**cadenza**: Virtuoso music designed to show off a singer's or an instrumental soloist's technical ability.

**Classical musical style**: Designation given to works of the later 18th century, characterized by clear melodic lines, balanced form, and emotional restraint. The style is brilliantly exemplified by the music of Franz Joseph Haydn.

**concerto**: Musical composition for orchestra and soloist(s) typically in three movements.

**consonance**: Two or more notes sounded together that do not require resolution.

**dissonance**: Two or more notes sounded together that require resolution.

**exposition**: Opening section of a fugue or sonata-form movement in which the main theme(s) are introduced.

**musical form**: Overall formulaic structure of a composition, such as sonata form; also the smaller divisions of the overall structure, such as the development section.

**overture**: Music that precedes an opera or play, often played as an independent concert piece.

**pedal note**: Pitch sustained for a long period of time against which other changing material is played. A pedal harmony is a sustained chord serving the same purpose.

**polyrhythm**: The simultaneous use of contrasting rhythms.

**polytonality**: The simultaneous use of two or more different keys (major and/or minor) or modes.

**Requiem**: Mass for the dead, traditionally in nine specific sections.

**rythmic asymmetry**: Rhythms that do not use regular accents.

**short score**: Two- or three-staff score that can be played on the piano and serves as the basis for a full orchestral score.

**sonata**: Piece of music typically in three or four movements, composed for a piano (piano sonata) or a piano plus one instrument (violin sonata, for example).

**sonata form**: Structural formula characterized by thematic development; usually used for the first movement of a sonata, symphony, or concerto.

**string quartet**: (1) Ensemble of four stringed instruments: two violins, viola and cello; (2) Composition for such an ensemble.

**symphony**: Large-scale instrumental composition for orchestra, containing several movements. The Viennese Classical symphony typically had four movements.

**voice**: A range or register, commonly used to refer to the four melodic ranges: soprano, alto, tenor, and bass.

# Biographical Notes

**Ansermet, Ernest** (1883–1969). Swiss conductor who organized the prestigious Orchestre de la Suisse Romande in Geneva, Switzerland, in 1918. Stravinsky introduced him to Serge Diaghilev and he became conductor of Diaghilev's Ballets Russes. He conducted the premiere of Stravinsky's ballet *Pulcinella* in May 1920.

**Cocteau, Jean** (1889–1963). French author and artist who wrote the libretto for Stravinsky's *Oedipus Rex* (1927).

**Craft, Robert** (1923– ). American conductor and writer who became a close friend and colleague of Stravinsky. In 1972, Craft published a biography of Stravinsky based on his twenty-five-year diary about his friendship with the composer.

**Diaghilev, Serge** (1872–1929). Russian impresario whose name is linked with many fine composers and artists. He established the famous ballet company *Les Ballets Russes* in Paris and commissioned Stravinsky to write *The Firebird*, *Petrouchka*, and *The Rite of Spring* ballet scores. Diaghilev's significance lies in his abandonment of classical ballet choreography for what would become the origins of modern dance.

**Dushkin, Samuel** (1891–1976). Polish-American violinist who studied with Leopold Auer and Fritz Kreisler. He collaborated with Stravinsky on the composer's Violin Concerto and was the soloist for the work's premiere in Berlin in 1931.

**Fokine, Mikhail** (1880–1942). Russian dancer and one of the most important and influential choreographers of the 20$^{th}$ century. He became choreographer for Diaghilev's Ballets Russes in 1909 and choreographed Stravinsky's ballets *The Firebird* (1910) and *Petrouchka* (1911).

**Maritain, Jacques** (1882–1973). French philosopher whose *Arts et Scholastique* was an influence on Stravinsky's artistic and musical views.

**Monteux, Pierre** (1875–1964). French-born American conductor who became famous for conducting modern ballets with Diaghilev's Ballets Russes. He led the world premieres of Stravinsky's *Petrouchka*, *The Rite of Spring*, and *Le Rossignol*. He was conductor of several American orchestras, including the Boston Symphony Orchestra, and of the Metropolitan Opera. He became a naturalized U.S. citizen in 1942.

**Nijinsky, Vaslav** (1890–1950). Russian dancer who joined Diaghilev's Ballets Russes in 1909 and was considered a highly original choreographer. He was the choreographer for Stravinsky's ballet *The Rite of Spring* (1913).

**Nosenko, Katerina (Katya)** (1881–1939). Stravinsky's cousin and first wife. They were married in 1906.

**Rimsky-Korsakov, Nicolai** (1844–1908). Russian nationalist composer whose music, with its use of the Russian idiom and oriental-sounding melodies, had a profound influence on the young Stravinsky. He gave Stravinsky early tutoring in composition.

**Stravinsky, Fyodor** (1843–1902). Stravinsky's father and a Russian bass of Polish descent. He was a member of the Russian Imperial Opera in St. Petersburg and became one of the greatest Russian basses, famous for his powerful voice and dramatic abilities, especially in heroic and comic roles.

**Sudeykin, Vera** (1888–1983). Stravinsky's second wife; they married in 1940 after an affair that lasted seventeen years.

# Bibliography

Antheil, George. *Bad Boy of Music*. Hutchinson, 1949.

Asafyev, Boris, translated by Richard French. *A Book about Stravinsky*. University of Michigan Press, 1982.

Bater, J. *St. Petersburg: Industrialization and Change*. Edward Arnold, 1976.

Benois, Alexander. *Reminiscences of the Russian Ballet*. Putnam, 1941.

Boucourechliev, Andre, translated by Martin Cooper. *Stravinsky*. Victor Gollancz, 1987.

Craft, Robert, ed. *Stravinsky: Selected Correspondence*. Faber and Faber, 1985.

Drummond, J. *Speaking of Diaghilev*. Faber and Faber, 1997.

Ecksteins, Modris. *The Rites of Spring*. Anchor Books, 1989.

Karsavina, Tamara. *Theatre Street*. London, 1981.

Laloy, L. *La Musique Retrouvee*. Plon, 1928.

Lederman, M., ed. *Stravinsky in the Theater*. Da Capo, 1975.

Leibowitz, H. A., ed. *Musical Impressions: Selections from Paul Rosenfeld's Criticism*. Hill and Wang, 1969.

Lesure, F., ed. *Claude Debussy: Correspondence 1884–1918*. Hermann, 1993.

Libman, Lillian. *And Music at the Close: Stravinsky's Last Years*. Macmillan, 1972.

Maritain, Jacques. *Art et Scholastique*. Paris, 1920.

Nabokov, Nicholas. *Old Friends and New Music*. Hamish Hamilton, 1951.

Rolland, Romain. *Journal of the War Years*. Edition Albin Michel, 1952.

Slonimsky, Nicholas. *Lexicon of Musical Invective*. University of Washington Press, 1975.

Stravinsky, Igor. *Chronicle of My Life*. Victor Gollancz, 1936.

Stravinsky, Igor, and Robert Craft. *Conversations with Igor Stravinsky*. University of California Press, 1958/1980.

———. *Dialogues*. University of California Press, 1961/1982.

———. *Expositions and Developments*. University of California Press, 1959/1981.

———. *Memories and Commentaries*. University of California Press, 1959/1981.

Stravinsky, Vera, and Robert Craft. *Stravinsky in Pictures and Documents*. Simon and Schuster, 1978.

Taruskin, Richard. *Stravinsky and the Russian Traditions*, Volumes 1 and 2. University of California Press, 1996.

Walsh, Stephen. *Stravinsky: A Creative Spring, 1882–1934*. Knopf, 1999.

Wenborn, Neil. *The Illustrated Lives of Great Composers: Stravinsky*. Music Sales Corp., New York, 1999.

White, Eric Walter. *Stravinsky: The Composer and His Work*. University of California Press, 1969.

Zilbershteyn, I., and V. Samkov, eds. *Serge Diaghilev.* Moscow, 1982.

# Notes

# Notes

# Notes

# Notes

# Notes

**Notes**

# Notes